Copyright 2012

ISBN-13: 978-1728675800

D1800146

TABLE OF CONTENTS

INTRODUCTION

Give me a stock clerk with a goal, and I will give you someone who will make history. Give me someone without a goal, and I will give you a stock clerk.—J.C. Penny

Have you ever wanted to accomplish something, but were unsure how to begin? Perhaps you started something, but couldn't figure out the right actions to take. Maybe you began taking action and nothing happened. The absence of a worthwhile outcome caused you to give up before you even got started.

Sometimes trying to accomplish a task or a goal can be like trying to find your way out of a large and confusing maze. You know where you are. You know where you want to go; however, the route between *here* and *there* is shrouded in mystery and worse, fear.

Well, your fear and confusion are about to pack their bags and head off into the sunset. That is because this book is going to take you by the hand and show you step-by-step how to achieve most anything. That's right—most anything.

You see, achievement is very much a process of moving from one place to another, just like the maze described above. If you don't know the route that leads to your destination, you'll just keep wandering in circles.

Ah, but what if someone gave you a map, a map with turn-by-turn directions that told you precisely where to go and which route to take while leading you easily down the maze? You'd be far more likely to succeed with that information.

Unfortunately, a map written by someone else can help you only so much. Unless the person creating the map understands your unique position in life—your strengths, weaknesses, skills, and lack thereof—any direction they provide will be basic. It will not be tailored to your needs. The map will not focus on you and what you want to accomplish.

Still, there is a solution. What if you had a personalized map? A map that took you through an easy step-by-step process to show you how to create action steps, overcome hurdles, and objectively evaluate your progress—all tailored to you?

With goal setting, this map is possible. Goal setting gives you that plus more. It will guide you in developing your own personally focused and targeted map, a map that will lead you to wherever you decide to go.

CHAPTER 1 – WHAT IS GOAL SETTING?

If you don't know where you are going, you'll end up someplace else.—Yogi Berra

Goal setting is the process of defining specific, measurable, and time-targeted objectives. You figure out your desires, you write them down, then you work on achieving them. This is the essence of the technique.

The ability to define and articulate your goals clearly is the single most important skill you can develop to achieve the success you desire. If you don't have a destination, how will you know where to go? If you set a destination, but your description is vague, how will you know if you have arrived?

Unfortunately, in our society, the word *goal* has a bad reputation. It is a word associated with commitments, responsibilities, and hard work. For some, it even reminds them of all the times they failed to reach their goals. Although this word has some negative connotations, setting and writing down goals is vital to any success. Below we discuss the reasons why.

BENEFITS AND IMPORTANCE OF GOAL SETTING

For starters, any time you set a goal, in a sense, a switch flips on within your mind that helps you notice opportunities that you never noticed before— opportunities instrumental in the attainment of your goal. Remember the last time you went to buy a car? Once you decided which model to buy, you started seeing them everywhere. Prior to flipping on that switch, you never noticed that model, even though they were always on the road with you. Establishing a goal works the same way. You become aware of options and choices you never knew existed. Opportunities could be staring you in the face, but you would never know.

Moreover, as humans, we naturally have many desires. The problem is that many of our desires conflict with each other. This means that fulfilling one desire requires giving up another. For example, say you desire to have a promotion at work, and at the same time, you desire the ability to enjoy your life. There may be a conflict there because if a promotion increases your responsibilities, that may put more pressure and stress on you, consequently decreasing the quality of your life. In relationships, many people who want to find that special someone can't because they still have a need to date other people. As you can see, sometimes fulfilling one desire means giving up another.

When you are faced with conflicting desires like this, instead of moving toward any specific want, you remain stagnant. Susan Jeffers talks about this dilemma in her bestseller *Feel the Fear and Do It Anyway*. As one of her students lamented, *Sometimes I feel like the proverbial donkey between two bales of hay—unable to decide which one I want, and in the meantime, starving to death.*

However, when you work through the goal setting steps, you find out what you want in life and figure out the things that you are willing to let go. As a result, you are not tugged in every which way by your conflicting desires. And when you narrow in on what you want, you have a destination. When you have a destination, it is easier to pick the right road. As a result, you spend less time and energy getting there. On the other hand, without goals or a destination, you are like a laser guided missile without any laser to guide you.

In addition to letting go of the chains that pull you in every direction, another benefit of goal setting is that it helps you steer away from circumstances you want to avoid in life. There are two types of people in this world—those who work toward what they want and those who work to avoid what they don't want. Most unsuccessful people in this world rarely focus on what they want. Instead, they spend their lives trying to avoid situations they don't want. They spend all their time and energy not wanting to *be rejected*, not wanting to *be broke*, or not wanting to *have bad things happen*.

It is good not to want negative things in your life, but always trying to avoid unwanted circumstances makes it difficult to move towards your desire. Imagine getting into a cab, for instance, and telling the driver all the places you don't want him to take you. He might take you to a place you like, or he might not. It works the same here. It's great to know that you don't want *debt* or a *stressful job*, but unless you communicate what it is that you *do* want, more than likely, you will be moving from one bad situation to the next.

This is where goal setting comes in. Setting goals helps you figure out what you want. By narrowing in on your aspirations, you fill the ambiguous void with a target. And when you work to move yourself toward that target, as a consequence, you automatically steer clear of negative situations you want to avoid in life. Moving toward the positive inherently moves you away from the negative. It happens naturally.

More importantly, goals allow you to take control. Instead of living life by chance, you live by choice. You choose your own outcome and select your own course of action. Again, unsuccessful people live life by chance. They don't do anything to take responsibility for their lives. Instead of thinking about what they would like out of life, they wait around for things to happen. They think the perfect job, person, or offer will come knocking on their door. When no one knocks, they get upset at the world.

There is no reason, though, to get upset. With goal setting, you choose what you want out of life. You determine what short-term and long-term goals you need to make that happen. Then you break them down into smaller and manageable targets that you complete on your way to success. This way, you don't wait around for things to happen. You create your own destiny.

Lastly, the greatest benefit of goal setting is that it gives you the precious ability to examine your life in the big picture. As a society on the go, we tend to get caught in a daily routine of completing tasks, setting schedules, and trying to make ends meet. We never get a chance to step outside this routine to see if we are on the right road. We make the mistake of thinking our active lifestyle is progress. However, without some sort of destination to guide our actions, our active, on-the-go lifestyle creates only an active, on-the-go lifestyle.

With goal setting, you step outside of this motion-cycle and look at your life in the big picture. You determine where you are and where you want to go. As mentioned, when you know where you want to go, you can set a plan of action to get there, instead of spinning round and round in your routine.

These are just a few of the many benefits of goal setting. To quickly summarize, goal setting opens your mind to new opportunities, eliminates conflicting desires, naturally steers you away from negative circumstances, helps you to see your life in the big picture, and most important of all, it puts you in the driver's seat of your life.

As you can see, goal setting is a robust tool for achievement. Sometimes the outcomes seem magical, but it is not magic. It is the power within you to achieve the things you want in life. Goal setting simply taps you into that power.

Now that you understand the potential of this tool, let's go deeper into the process. Next, you'll learn about timeframes and how they apply to goal setting.

CHAPTER 2 – TIME FRAMES

If you fail to plan, you plan to fail.—Harvey MacKay

It's helpful to see goals in three timeframes: immediate, intermediate, and long-term. Each timeframe has its own set of demands, strengths and weaknesses. Let's discuss these in more detail.

IMMEDIATE

Immediate goals refer to the next few weeks. They are concerned with the exigencies of day-to-day life. These are things that you cannot put off to a later time and are typically the easiest to measure, or at the very least, easiest to determine when you have done your best.

On the most basic level, getting food and shelter are immediate needs or goals. Giving a great presentation at work can be an important immediate goal as well. Many intermediate to long-term goals can be broken into smaller chunks of immediate goals. These immediate goals drive what you need to do day to day to achieve your distant desires.

INTERMEDIATE

Intermediate goals refer to the next few months. Though you may have heard the famous marketing slogan *Where do you want to be in X years*, you probably haven't been asked where you want to be in the next few months. Intermediate goals are more challenging because they typically depend upon reaching the immediate goals first, but also because it is more difficult to plan six months ahead. Nevertheless, these goals are just as important for success.

Intermediate goals help you prepare for your bigger goals. You could, for example, give yourself six months to realize an understanding of this book and start practicing what it says. You may want to move to another job, and it could easily take you three or four months to get your resume and recommendations in order. When your intermediate goals are well-thought out, they are a very powerful tool that can help you through all sorts of trials and difficulties.

LONG-TERM

Long-term goals refer to desires that will be reached in the next few years and longer. These goals are by far the most typical. When self-help gurus preach about goal setting, they usually preach about setting long-term goals.

An important aspect of long-term goals is that these goals rarely, if ever, take into consideration what you will learn along the way. It's difficult to predict your future thoughts or knowledge. You may discover, for example, while you are working toward becoming a millionaire, that having a good home life is far more important than your bank account. Or you may realize that being in good health is more important than becoming a top athlete. Still, this level of planning is important because it gives you an overall direction to your decision-making and provides coherence to your life that you would not have otherwise.

Being able to differentiate the timeframe of a goal into immediate, intermediate, or long-term is a helpful template. It will enable you to measure your progress and achieve personal satisfaction once you have successfully met your goal. Keep these timeframes in mind as you dive into the goal-setting process in the next chapter.

CHAPTER 3 – DISCOVER WHAT YOU WANT

What would you attempt to do if you knew you could not fail?—Robert Schuller

There are two parts to goal setting. First is figuring out *what* you want. This requires taking the time to reflect seriously and systematically on the things you would like to have and achieve in life. Only when you have a clear target of *what* can you put yourself in motion to get it.

The second part of goal setting deals with *how*. It revolves around figuring out *how* you are going to achieve that what you want. This requires analyzing the goal, breaking it down, and creating an action plan. It also requires getting yourself to take action and staying committed.

This chapter will focus on the *what* aspect of goal setting. It will help you look at where you are in life and guide you in discovering where you want to go. We recommend that you not set goals for the sake of setting goals. Instead, set goals to achieve something you desire. Otherwise, you may lose your motivation to get it done, and this can create feelings of failure and disappointment.

So, what do you want?

Before you answer, know that your goals are personal and can be anything you choose. You may wish to fly a plane, see the Seven Wonders of the World, direct a movie, or become an athlete, artist or the CEO of a company.

Your conquests don't have to be this grand. They can be as simple as spending time with the kids, calling your parents more often, getting organized, finding a mate, landing a new job or getting better grades.

You can also set goals to develop yourself as a person. This can include conquering fears, overcoming depression, gaining confidence, feeling happy, becoming spiritual, improving memory, or learning a new skill.

You might even set a chain of goals, going from one to the next, from lower to higher.

As you ponder on potential goals, realize that there is often a big disconnect between what we *think* we want or are *told* to want, and what truly fulfills us. Our expectations are rarely in line with reality. Our mind has a tendency to convince us that a specific object or situation will make us feel a certain way, when it won't.

For example, have you ever walked into a department store and caught the attention of a stunning dress or a fantastic pair of shoes? As soon as the item catches your attention, you become consumed by the thought of having it. Your mind runs amuck as you imagine how great life will be with that dress or shoe. You replay numerous scenarios of everyone staring and commenting on your stunning look.

If you are a guy reading this, your experience is likely in reference to an expensive piece of gadget or electronic device. As soon as you see it, you envision how complete its possession will make you. This device will manage all your tasks, schedules, and completely organize your life. It will be so great, you will be so efficient. It is sure to make all your peers envious and skyrocket your popularity with them.

Then you make the purchase or place the order. You wait for it to arrive or to put to use. Once you do, however, the object or situation doesn't change your life the way you initially thought it would. Not only that, but it doesn't even change your mood. Maybe you engage in a bit of excitement for a few days because you were happy to have that which you so craved. Shortly after, though, your life is back to normal, and your mind on the next big wish or want— unfulfilled and back to its initial state.

From these experiences, it is easy to see that as humans we are very poor predictors of the future and how we will react to it. As a result of this disconnect, we are rarely in touch with our honest desires. We might think a situation will make us happy, when in fact it won't, or we might dread the consequences of an outcome, even though the result might be long-term benefit and lasting joy.

In order to bridge this gap between your needs and wants, we have provided an exercise below. This exercise poses an important set of questions. The questions will kick-start your thinking about from where you derive pleasure and the things that bring you joy.

Go through the questions and answer them as accurately as you can. Don't hold back or suppress your responses. Answer each one as honestly and truthfully as possible. As you answer, be open to the fact that what you want may end up being completely different from what you originally thought.

- Begin with the end in mind—where would you like to be in five, ten, or twenty years? If everything could fall into place, how would you see your future?

- Answer the age-old question—what would you do if you had a million dollars? Let's make this question more thought provoking—what would you do if you had a billion dollars?

• If you could design the perfect life, how would it look? What would you add? What would you take out?

• If you could go back in time, what would you do differently, what would you change? Would you go back to school or would you pick a different occupation?

• If you could eliminate all resistance, suppose you are secure, confident, and have no fears, what is the first thing you would do?

• As a child, what did you most enjoy doing?

• If judgment from others had no effect on you, how would you change your life?

• Imagine yourself in the distant future when you are old and grey. As you look back at your life, how would you liked to have been known or remembered, or what would you liked to have done?

• Lastly, if you no longer had the need to feed or defend your ego, how would you proceed?

As mentioned, this questionnaire should get you thinking about *what* truly fulfills you. The answers you come up with can be interpreted as desires worth pursuing. Take these answers and analyze them in terms of goals you can set.

GOAL GUIDELINES

Now that you have some goals in mind, think about them with respect to the following. Adhering to these guidelines will ensure that your goals will generate the level of motivation and tenacity needed to see them through.

Self-selected

Make sure you pick a goal that you want, not one that someone wants for you. You increase the likelihood of staying committed to goals that you select for your own reasons, instead of ones that are selected for you by other people.

Reasonable

Ensure that you allow for reasonable time frames to achieve your goals. There are no limits to what you can achieve, but if you've never played basketball in your life, making the varsity basketball team with two weeks of practice is not a reasonable goal.

Slightly Challenging

You need to strike the right balance with your goal; it must be challenging, but accomplishable. If your goal is too difficult, you may become overwhelmed. On the other hand, if it is too easy, you won't find it rewarding and will stop paying attention to it.

Specific

Be specific. To own a three-bedroom house with a two-car garage in the north suburbs of Chicago is a clearer target for your mind than merely saying *to own my own home*.

Measurable

It is easier to stay committed if you can measure progress. If you set a goal to increase sales by 10 percent, and your sales are up by 5, that is measurable progress. If you want to lose weight, setting a goal of losing 25 pounds is more measurable than merely saying you want to be thin.

Positive

Say what you want to achieve instead of what you want to avoid. Say: *I will attend all classes* instead of *I won't miss any classes*. When I say, *don't think of a pink cow*, what is the first thing that pops up in your mind? A pink cow. Your mind doesn't hear the words *won't* and *no*. It works the same when wording goals.

For example, if you word a goal of *not missing any classes*, your mind automatically visualizes you missing classes. This is not what you want your mind to do. You want your mind to visualize your true outcome. You do that by stating your goals in the positive.

Deadline

Set a date by which you want to accomplish your goal. Deadlines will make you more serious about your ambition. Otherwise, you might find yourself postponing your efforts to get started.

When you set deadlines, do so appropriately. Remember that some goals may take years to accomplish, while others can take as little as a day. Also, some goals don't have a completion deadline, but rather a deadline to start something. For example, a goal to spend more time with the kids is something you start doing by a specific date, as opposed to something you finish.

These are the guidelines that make your goals more effective. Not all of your goals will fit into every guideline, but the more guidelines you can apply, the clearer your goal.

Clarity is vital. A vague idea will not cut it. You'll just end up wasting your time. Not only will you be confused about how to accomplish it, but you also won't be able to track your progress.

Here are examples of some generic goals and how you can use the above guidelines to make them clear:

- **To get a raise**—*To get a 10% raise by the end of the year*

- **To reduce my workload**—*To reduce my workload at my job by turning down extra assignments*

- **To lose 50 pounds by next month**—*To lose 25 pounds in 6 months*

- **To write a book**—*To write a mystery novel by May 30, 2018*

- **To take a vacation**—*To take a yachting trip and visit the Alps in the summer of 2015*

- **To spend time with the kids**—*To spend at least one hour each day with the kids starting this weekend*

- **To go back to school**—*To have a marketing degree from Columbia University by June 2018*

- **To improve health**—*To improve how I look and feel and to have more energy with noticeable results in two months*

Notice how each reworded goal is clear and to the point. These goals are personal, specific and reasonable. They are not vague statements like *I want to be rich* or outlandish efforts to *lose 50 pounds by next month*. They narrow in on what you want as well as when you want it.

Now that you understand how to word goals, take the desires that were revealed in the above questionnaire and put together some goals you would like to have, have happen, or achieve. If you uncovered many desires, pick a few of the more important ones. In the beginning, you might want to start with ones that are easy and simple to implement. This way you have practice getting accustomed to the process.

Then write your goals down. This is the most important part of goal setting. Studies show that people who write down their goals are 80 percent more likely to achieve them. In essence, if your goal is not in writing, it is not really a goal. It might be a great desire, but it's not a goal.

My goals are . . .

To: _____

To: _____

To: _____

To: _____

To: _____

ANALYZE COST AND BENEFITS

Once you've figured out what you want and you've used the above guidelines to write down some realistic, time-targeted objectives, it's time to think about the benefits and costs of your goal. Benefits are your motivations for the goal, and costs are what you will be giving up and the effort that will be required to achieve the goal.

Every success has a cost or downside. That is, to have one thing almost always means you have to give up something else. To understand the information in this book requires you to spend some time reading it, time that you now don't have to spend with your family or friends. Time spent with your family and friends is time you could be using to meet your monetary goals. Time you spend trying to meet your monetary goals is time you cannot use to catch up on fun activities. I can go on and on, but you get the picture.

The downside of having a dream realized goes beyond lost time. It means giving up other things. For example, if you want to become a celebrity, that could mean giving up, to a certain degree, your privacy. If you want to climb the corporate ladder, that may involve trading genuine friends for *business friends*, friends who may or may not be there when the going gets tough or be spiritually fulfilling.

This concept also applies to material possessions. Having more *things* requires putting in the effort to maintain, take care of, and protect those things, which can come at a cost. Again, I can go on, but you understand what I am trying to get at. The old adage *be careful what you wish for, because you just might get it* certainly applies to goal-setting.

The point is, there is always a cost or downside to realizing a goal. People who fail to achieve their goals do so because they fail to understand this. They get so excited by the thought of having their desire fulfilled, they miss the fact that there will be drawbacks. Because they overlook the drawbacks, they do not properly assess whether or not the benefits they expect from the goal will outweigh its cost. So when the going gets tough or they realize they have to make compromises, they give up. In essence, they fail before they ever begin.

To make sure this does not happen to you, it is important to do a cost benefit analysis. By doing this, you determine beforehand what it will take to accomplish your goal and the possible difficulties that may arise. This way you can prepare for the difficulties in advance or decide ahead of time whether or not the goal is worth pursuing. Film writer Sidney Howard said, *One-half of knowing what you want is knowing what you must give up before you get it*.

With that said, take each goal on your list and write down its benefits and costs. For example, if your goal is to become a lawyer, the benefits might be the prestige, income and the knowledge that you might gain. On the other hand, you will have to spend 3 years in law school, pay for your education and possibly come out of school with a lot of debt. In addition, a law degree is not a guarantee of easy money. You still have to get up and go to work day-in and day-out to earn a steady stream of paychecks; therefore working as a lawyer may involve more effort than you are willing to put in. Take a few moments and think about why you want the goal and what you will have to give up to achieve it.

Benefits	Costs
1.	1.
2.	2.
3.	3.
4.	4.
5.	5.
6.	6.
7.	7.

Once you finish listing the benefits and costs, ask yourself if the benefits outweigh the costs for you to commit to this endeavor. If you can honestly answer *yes*, you're on your way. If not, try your hand on something else or modify the goal in such a way that you can still commit to pursuing it.

In addition to evaluating the downside, another advantage of doing a cost benefit analysis is that it helps you determine if your goal is an end or simply a means to an end. Meaning, did you choose your goal because you thought it would help you achieve something else? For example, if you decide you want to be a lawyer, and the reason is so you could be financially stable, then your goal is not really *to be a lawyer*. It is *to be financially stable*. Becoming a lawyer is just a means to that specific end.

For right now, concentrate on the end—what it is that you truly desire. You will work on the means in the next chapter when you create an action plan. To determine if your goal is an end or simply a means to an end, look at the benefits and decide if this is something you really want, or does it just represent something you want? If it is the latter, figure out what the goal represents to you.

That could be a really easy answer, and in many cases, it will be. On the other hand, you might find that the goal you've set truly represents a state or condition such as stability, security, health or happiness. In that case, the state or condition is the goal. You might then choose to change how you go about creating the condition. That is, instead of pursuing a degree in law to achieve *financial stability*, you might consider less difficult or more enjoyable alternatives. Or you might decide that the goal you have picked is the right one for you. Either way, if your goal feels like an end, go with it.

Congratulations. You've just taken the first step in transforming your desires into reality. While this step is a bit lengthy, it's meant to help you zero in on a clear and specific target, one that will help you understand what you want to achieve while making you conscious of the effort needed to achieve it.

Initially, all these instructions might seem overwhelming. Their purpose, however, is not to overwhelm you. It is to help you get what you really want in the shortest time possible. This step-by-step process is the most effective way to do that.

Again, congratulations! You're now on an exciting path to creating a better life for yourself.

CHAPTER 4 – ACHIEVE IT FASTER THAN YOU THINK POSSIBLE

Our goals can only be reached through a vehicle of a plan, in which we must fervently believe, and upon which we must vigorously act. There is no other route to success. —Stephen A. Brennan

The last chapter started off stating that goal setting can be broken into two parts. The first part involved discovering what you want. It entailed analyzing yourself and figuring out from where you derive fulfillment. It also entailed scrutinizing your desires to determine if they would truly fulfill you or if they were something society convinced you to have.

The second part deals with attaining your goal. This is where you achieve it faster than you think possible. In this chapter, you will take your goal and develop a plan of action. You will also learn about overcoming fears and habits and getting yourself to taking action on your plan. More importantly, you will learn how to maintain momentum to see your goal to the end.

STEP 1 – CREATE AN ACTION PLAN

Now that you've specified your goal, it's time to think about the action steps that will lead you to the finish line. When we build something, whether it is an automobile or a house, it is designed and planned out before the project is started. Can you imagine asking construction workers to build a house without a plan? How likely is it that the house would be assembled correctly? Just as construction workers need blueprints, a goal-setter needs action steps—making the phone call, attending seminars and scheduling tasks—that lay the ground work for what they need to do today, tomorrow, next week and next month to realize their goal.

Action steps are useful because they help you figure out how to get started. Often people fail to take action simply because they don't know where to start. If this is you, know that this feeling of uncertainty is common and can be easily managed with a well thought-out plan of action. Your action plan will break larger goals into smaller, more manageable objectives that will give you a clear starting point.

Action steps are also practical because they immediately tell you if your goal is too big or unrealistic, at least for the present. As you are listing your action steps, you might realize you are getting in over your head or that you can't complete everything within the deadline you set. If that is the case, here is where you can make adjustments accordingly.

Knowledge

First, begin by identifying and writing down additional information achieving your goal will require. This can include performing research, reading books, taking courses, or obtaining specialized expertise. Are there specific people from whom you could seek advice?

Don't be afraid or too proud to seek professional assistance. If your goal is to lose 25 pounds, it would be wise to see a personal trainer, physician and nutritionist before beginning so they can assess your needs and guide you to adopt proper diet and exercise habits. It might also be beneficial to research and read up on weight loss in books and articles, getting ideas about how others have achieved their weight loss goals and what they did to stay motivated and make the journey easier.

What additional information does my goal require? Record this below:

_____

_____

_____

_____

_____

_____

Obstacles

Next, list potential obstacles. Obstacles are barriers that prevent you from starting the goal now. If your goal is to lose 25 pounds, an obstacle preventing you from starting could be that you don't know how to prepare healthy meals. Another obstacle might be that you lack the necessary equipment to exercise.

Obstacles also include barriers and distractions that will interfere with you reaching your goal in the future. If your friends and family are overweight, their lack of motivation and support can be a barrier that may create difficulty in the future. Maintaining enthusiasm might also be an issue that can get in the way down the road.

In order to achieve a goal, you need to understand what is standing in your way. This way you can deal with it before it becomes a problem. You don't need to worry about the trivial obstacles. Focus only on those ones that require a course of action to fix.

What are the obstacles that I need to overcome? Record this below:

_____

_____

_____

_____

_____

_____

Action Plan

Finally, based on the above information, develop an action plan. Your action plan is the means to get you to your end destination. It lays out how you are going to gain the desired knowledge, overcome the obstacles, and ultimately reach your objective. Make sure to concentrate on productive actions—the actions that will carry the most power, the actions that will lead to the greatest results.

Using the weight-loss example, an action plan of losing 25 pounds may look as follows:

1. See nutritionist to learn proper eating habits.

2. Schedule personal training sessions to learn correct ways to exercise.

3. Visit doctor to ensure body is healthy for diet and exercise.

4. Read books on how to lose weight.

5. Learn to prepare healthy meals.

6. Buy exercise equipment or sign up for a gym membership.

7. Listen to motivational tapes to maintain drive and enthusiasm.

8. Run 30 minutes every Monday, Wednesday and Friday.

9. Go to aerobics class every Saturday.

10. Decrease food intake to 1,800 calories/day.

11. Reduce fat intake to 45 grams/day.

The above is a sample action plan for losing weight. Notice, the first four action steps address the knowledge one needs to gain. The next three address potential obstacles to overcome. The last four steps focus specifically on losing weight. When you are creating your action plan, make sure to address these items.

Also notice that action steps come in two forms. Some steps require that you take action only once, after which you can cross off your list. Other steps require that you repeat the action over and over, so you never really cross it off. For example, visiting a doctor for a check-up is a step that you probably need to perform only once. On the other hand, decreasing your food intake and exercising are continuing actions you will have to do over and over until you meet your objective. Be cognizant of this so you can prepare your schedule accordingly.

More importantly, realize that each action step can be broken down further into smaller and more manageable steps. For example, action item 10. Decrease food intake to 1,800 calories/day is fairly broad. It doesn't address how it can be achieved. So you can break it down further with details like what foods to eat, what foods to avoid, a plan for each meal, etc. Break each item further and further to give yourself a clear outline that you can follow.

Approach each action item and sub-item like a mini goal. Follow the same guidelines as your main goal as much as possible: make them realistic and specific, set a deadline, and more importantly, write them down.

The steps I will take to reach this goal are:

1. _____

2. _____

3. _____

4. _____

5. _____

6. _____

7. _____

8. _____

9. _____

10. _____

STEP 2 – AFFIRMATIONS

Most authors and personal development experts guarantee their success strategies to bring results regardless of the person. In the end, these strategies work for only a handful of people. The reason is because any time you set out to create change, you go into battle. You go into battle with your internal mechanisms. These mechanisms include *habits* you've ingrained over the years, *fears* you have about taking action, and *beliefs* about your ability to succeed and be successful in life. Your habits, fears, and beliefs are inner processes that can keep you from forging ahead in life.

In other words, your struggles and current situation, for the most part, are not a result of some external force that is oppressing you or keeping you down. They are a result of internal mechanisms that make it difficult for you to move forward. These mechanisms create a psychic wall that not only slow your progress, but in many cases, cause you to sabotage your own efforts. You can't see this wall, but it is there tripping you at every opportunity. When people say, *you are your own worst enemy*, this is what they mean.

In order to successfully achieve your goals, it is crucial to tear down this wall. You need to break free from stale habits that are keeping you stuck in your old routine, overcome fears and apprehensions that are holding you back from taking action, and more importantly, you need to change negative beliefs about yourself and your abilities from *I can't* to *I can*. Doing so will remove many of the obstacles getting in the way of your goals.

There are many ways to break down your physic wall, but I've found the quickest and easiest way is through the use of affirmations. Affirmations are statements that you declare to be true. More specifically, they are statements that you want to make or have be true. For example, if you are shy and insecure and want to fix this quality, you would repeat affirmations like *I am confident and outgoing* or *I am secure and self-assured*. Used this way, affirmations improve how you think and feel about yourself, as well as your ability to act.

Affirmations go beyond verbal statements. They also include visual images. That is because your mind processes thoughts both through words and pictures, so in addition to verbally affirming the outcomes you desire, you can visualize them. You can mentally picture yourself succeeding, performing well, or having the success you seek.

Next to knowing what you want, supporting your goals with affirmations is hands down the most important aspect of goal setting. It is also the primary reason that many achievement techniques fail. Affirmations free you from the prison of your inner programming. By applying affirmations to your goals on a regular basis, you neutralize the effects of restricting habits, fears, and beliefs while creating newer and better ones. Ones that empower you to set, plan for, and achieve the results you desire.

To assert affirmations effectively, first calm your mind and easing into a relaxed state. Then you repeat a set of verbal statements. Afterwards, visualize the end result. Following is an exercise that walks you through these steps.

Start by sitting or lying in a position that makes you comfortable. Breathe deeply and rhythmically. Inhale and exhale slowly. Picture your tense muscles slowly relaxing. Unknot those tight bunches and blow them out with your breath.

Now repeat each of the following statements ten times:

I enjoy setting goals.

Goals are fun and easy to achieve.

I am committed to accomplishing my goal of . . . .

Then affirm three or four statements specific to your goal that will help you stay active and committed to it. Here you can include statements that will address obstacles you need to overcome. For example, if you desire to lose weight, you might affirm:

I am eating healthy every day.

I am exercising regularly.

I have full control over what I eat, where I eat, and how I eat.

Each day, I am getting closer and closer to my ideal weight.

Finally, affirm three or four statements that represent the end result of your goal. If your goal is to lose weight, you probably want to look fit, be healthy, and have an attractive body. Thus you might repeat:

I am slender, fit, and trim.

I have an attractive, healthy body.

I am attaining and maintaining my ideal weight.

After you affirm each statement 10 times, visualize the end result of your goal. What does it look like? If your goal is to lose weight, envision how you want to look. What size jeans do you want to fit into? If your goal is good health, picture your body healthy and strong. Imagine your medical exam with positive outcomes and lab work showing healthy results. If your goal is to write a book, picture the finished manuscript and its cover and notice your name as the author. If you want to travel to Paris, visualize yourself enjoying your vacation there.

Give positive feelings to your words and pictures. Be optimistic. Flood yourself with pure, unadulterated belief in your ability to do this. Strip yourself of all negative sensations. Let go of heartaches and heartbreaks.

Your mind takes your mental statements and pictures as instructions to lead your future actions. By feeding your mind positive thoughts and images of goals in this way, you guide your actions in that direction. So, set aside a few minutes every day to do this exercise, preferably upon waking up in the morning and before going to sleep at night. At these times, your mind is the most calm and relaxed, allowing you to solidify your expectations and put yourself in the right mood as you go through the motions of your day.

Think of your goals as the seeds of your desire and your action plan as the water and sunshine vital for growth. With that, affirmations are the healthy dose of nutrients that will give your goals that extra edge to ensure they grow and develop to their fullest.

STEP 3 – TAKE ACTION

This step is to remind you that your goal will not manifest unless you take action. You're probably thinking, *that seems obvious*. As obvious as it seems, many people never really get around to taking action. They get stuck simply planning and dreaming.

Don't get caught in this phase. Planning and dreaming might make you feel like you're being productive and moving forward in life, but the most detailed and effective plan is worthless if you never put it into action. I'm sure you've heard the saying, *knowledge is power*. Knowledge is not power in of itself; applied knowledge is power. Only when knowledge is applied for a specific objective does it have power. With that said, once you have a plan and begin to affirm the success that you desire, get up off that chair and start applying your plan to realize your goals.

My personal experience shows that two main fears keep people from taking action. First, goal setting can feel overwhelming, especially in the beginning. When you start, there are so many tasks that you have to plan for, remember, and do, that it can overwhelm you. The list can feel like it is just too much or that you won't be able to handle it all.

This fear is common and natural. Anytime you embark to create change or any time you do something new, feelings of heavy load and pressure arise. You will second guess yourself, play *what if* scenarios, and over think and over analyze your decisions and actions. As I said, it's not only common, but very natural.

You can manage this fear by approaching the goal one step at a time. Take one action item and concentrate your efforts on completing and/or performing that one item. Don't beat yourself into thinking that you have to compete all the action items in one day or in one sitting. Also, don't think that all the tasks have to be done quickly, right away, and perfect the first time around. Take your time. Start with one of the steps, complete it, and then move to the next.

As you tackle each step, your list will get smaller and become more manageable. Quickly, you will reach a point where the only items remaining will be the ones requiring repetition, i.e. exercising regularly. As you start on these items, the more you do them, the easier they will get. They will internalize as habits and become a part of your daily routine. Just keep at it. Focus on one task or item before moving onto the next.

The other fear that keeps people from taking action is lack of experience. Often people feel as though they don't have the necessary information or knowledge to begin. They don't know what to do nor how. This causes them to feel unprepared. Since they feel unprepared, they put their efforts on becoming prepared. They spend all their time reading, understanding, charting, and learning about what to do, instead of going out and actually doing it. This is a form of procrastination called *creative avoidance*. It's looking for creative excuses or reasons to avoid take action on your plan.

To overcome inaction from lack of experience, realize that in most situations, you already know enough to get started. The additional knowledge *you think* you need can be gained only from the actual experience of going out there and doing it. Ray Bradbury's sums this up best in his mantra *jump, and you will find out how to unfold your wings as you fall*.

These are couple things to think about to help you overcome your fears of starting your goals. Unfortunately fear is an emotion. At times and for some people, no amount of logic or persuasion can change that feeling. I can sit here and logically write for hours about how *there is nothing to fear, but fear itself* and motivate you to not let fears stop you from taking action. But because it's an emotion, and not easily persuaded by logic, the feeling will persist. Nothing I or your friends and family or anyone else can say to change that. In fact, the emotion might be so strong, you will come up with reasons and excuses to counter any reassurance I or anyone might give you.

If you find yourself in this position, regrettably, there is nothing additional I can say. From the bottom of my heart, I wish I can give you the right set of words to inspire you to push past your fears. However, because you are dealing with an emotion, more words is not the answer. Not to mention, I'm sure over the years you've received more than your fair share of inspirational words from movies, books, graduation ceremonies, famous quotes, seminars, Oprah, friends, family, motivational speakers, church, celebrated stories, etc. If none of them have enabled you to act, additional words from me is not going to be of much use. You will have to find the inner strength you need on your own. Anything additional I say will likely only create more resistance and fuel for your fear.

If there is one thing I could say, it would be to realize that fear tends to be stronger when we are outside of it than when we are in it. Meaning, the feelings of fear are more intense when we are thinking about the possibility of something bad happening than after it has already happened or when the event causing fear is approaching than after it has arrived. As it relates to taking action on a goal, the feelings of fear are much more intense when you are thinking about taking action than when you are actually in action.

This happens because anytime we decide to do something new or different, our mind plays out all sorts of negative scenarios like *what if I fail*, *what if I am ridiculed, what if things don't go well*. This creates a lot of resistance and apprehension, which makes us want to give up before giving our goal the light of day.

However, once we step inside the fear and take action, it doesn't feel all that bad. In other words, by piercing through the fear, the feelings tend to ease up and dissolve rather quickly. Often you'll wonder what you were so afraid of all along. It's only when we are outside does it seem intimidating.

By taking the first step, less fear exists than before you took it. This makes it easier to take the second step. Taking the second step makes it easier to take the third, and so on. But unless you take the first step, you will be stuck in an eternal state of hesitation.

So whether you feel overwhelmed, unprepared, or have fear for any other reason, take the first step, even if it's a small step. Don't be scared. As you will notice, taking action is not always as scary as it seems to feel.

Once you take the first step, make sure to do something every day that brings you closer to realizing your goal. Pick at least one action item, no matter how small, to work on each day. Ask yourself, *what is the most important task I can complete today?* Day by day, chip away at your plan.

As you will notice, taking action quickly builds momentum. Just as chronic inaction can create a cycle of stagnation over time, being proactive can create a positive cycle that continues to grow. This becomes easier the more you do it. Eventually the action will seem almost effortless, and you will continue to empower and strengthen yourself with every step you take.

So don't put off the effort until tomorrow or next week or when the time is right. Start now. Do something right now to get yourself in motion. Even if it is midnight, find something on the action list that you can start right away. If you don't complete the action item today, at least you've started.

STEP 4 – REVIEW

At this point, you should have a clear, detailed plan for achieving your goal. You should know exactly what you want, have a list of specific action steps to take, and a general expectation about both the completion of your activities and the culmination of your goal.

Still, you're not done yet.

Once you are moving forward and working toward your goals, it is important to review them regularly. You can do this by taking a few minutes each morning to look at your written goals and plan of action. It's best to do this as soon as you get out of bed so you begin each day with them in mind. It's also a good idea to keep a list of your goals where you are likely to run into them regularly, perhaps in your purse or wallet, an office drawer you open often, or on your refrigerator.

There are couple reasons why the review process is important. First and foremost, it ensures you stay with your goals. It is very easy to set goals and then either forget about them or slowly move away. They can easily become faded memories lost in our daily routine. By having a schedule where you can look at and revisit your goals often, you are less likely to lose them in a sea of other priorities.

The other purpose of the review step is to help you assess your progress and determine if you are off target. If you are, you can figure out what you need to do to get back on track. The review process also helps you determine if there will be unexpected road blocks that are going to take you off course. If there will be, then you will have time to prepare for and act on them.

When you review, you should evaluate two things. First, evaluate your daily actions. Every one or two weeks, take a few moments to answer these questions:

• Are you sticking to your original plans?

• Could you improve upon your actions in any way?

• Have you had to move to Plan B at any time? If so, how did that work out for you?

• Can you see room for improvement in your original plans?

• Have you made any modifications to your action plans? If so, are they working better for you?

• Have your results met your expectations so far? If not, why not?

• What can you do to improve your results?

Second, evaluate your long-term progress. This can be done monthly or even quarterly. Every month or so, take a momentary step back and answer these questions:

• Are your plans moving you in the right direction?

• Is your ultimate goal still the same, or are you considering a change in direction?

• Can you think of any ways to improve upon your original plans?

• What are you learning about yourself through this process?

• Have you developed a stronger appreciation of any aspect of yourself?

• Which of your qualities and habits still need improvement?

• How can you begin to expand your potential and stretch your limits?

• Are you beginning to think of even larger goals you can achieve now?

Like any path, there are turns, detours and potholes. You must anticipate them and adjust your plan accordingly to maneuver around them.

There you have it. This is goal setting in a nutshell. You start by figuring out your heart's desires. Then, you create an action plan and charge your mind with positive affirmations. Next, you take action. Finally, you review your goals and action steps regularly to make sure you are on track. Every goal has a clearly defined route leading to its realization, and with a fair amount of planning and foresight, you can easily achieve your objectives.

See, that wasn't so bad. Within about 40 pages, you have gained powerful insight as to what you want out of life and how to get it in the most effective, least time-consuming way possible. No matter what goals you set now or in the future, you have an easy-to-duplicate formula that will help you achieve them.

Now, some might say that this process is either too linear or too simplified, but why shouldn't it be? Why complicate the process when it does not have to be? Someone once said, *truth is simple. If it were complicated, everyone would get it*.

Nonetheless, life is neither linear nor simple. There will be distractions that will take you of course. In the next chapter, we will discuss how to handle these distractions to ensure you stick with your goals to the end.

CHAPTER 5 – STAYING ON COURSE

I took the one less traveled by, and that has made all the difference.—Robert Frost

In a perfect world, you should easily be able to take your goals and action steps and follow them to the tee. However, we don't live in a perfect world. There will be distractions and diversions that will pull you away from your purpose. Some of these distractions will be external, while others will be internal.

In this chapter we will discuss ways to help you stay committed and show you what to do if you become distracted and fall off the path. More importantly, we will talk about when it is acceptable to leave your goals, and in effect, change paths.

We will start first with deadlines.

DEADLINES

If you can't meet a deadline you set, it is not the end of the world. Don't get bogged down and give up your efforts. Often, people will miss a target date for their goal and get discouraged. Realize that life happens. There will be moments in your journey when one area of your life requires more attention than another area, and you may miss a deadline.

Deadlines are important because they give you a sense of commitment and motivation. They urge you to stay focused, push yourself to work harder and smarter, and to be proactive in overcoming obstacles. However, deadlines can sometimes cause immense impatience and frustration, especially if things don't move along at the pace we expect.

Our expectations get us worked up more often than we'd like to admit. If we expect something to go well and it doesn't, we feel angry and disappointed. If we expect results by a certain date and the results do not materialize, we lose all hope and give up because it seems futile to continue. I'm sure you've experienced situations like these before—most of us have.

While it's good to set a timeline for the completion of your goal, it's best not to set it in stone. This way you will still have a feeling of urgency, yet you won't get hooked on the idea of having certain things happen at a certain time, especially if those things are largely out of your control.

Setting a deadline is important, but reaching the target you set for yourself is far more important. Suppose you set a goal to lose 25 pounds before summer, but you don't reach your goal until fall. As much as you would have loved to show off your beach body during the summer, did the date really matter? You accomplished your goal eventually and are now enjoying being thinner and healthier.

Don't give up, therefore, simply because you can't make a deadline. Just be sure to set realistic deadlines. Don't create more stress for yourself by taking on a massive project and expecting to complete it within a few days. Moderate, consistent actions will be more effective than getting burned out.

GOING OFF COURSE

There will be times when you momentarily lose your way and go off-course. Let's look at the weight loss example again. Instances may arise when you give in to temptation and gobble up that extra piece of pastry or that inviting scoop of ice cream. Even worse, you may ignore your exercise regimen for a week or two, maybe even longer.

What do most people do when this happens? They throw in the towel. They automatically assume that going off course means they have to give up the goal. Worse, they may assume that going off course means they don't have what it takes to achieve their goal. Both of these couldn't be farther from the truth.

Change is not an event, but a process. Change happens through a series of stages, and most successful self-changers fail at least once before they succeed. For most people, the process of change is not a straight path that takes them from one point to the next.

Successful self-changers usually follow a path that's more like a spiral. They move forward, go back to a previous stage, and move on to the next level of commitment one or more times before changing for good. You need to understand this cycle of change and how it will affect your goal. Otherwise, you risk throwing in the towel at every sign of challenge.

With that said, do not give up your goal just because you veered off course. Get back on the wagon and begin the journey from where you left off. Return to your course as soon as you can and continue with your action plan. Do not give in just because you fell by the wayside once or twice.

REWARD YOURSELF

Reward yourself for accomplishing your goals. When you work hard to reach an objective you've set, it's important to enjoy the by-products of your success. Whether it's sporting your improved figure at the beach, taking your family on a vacation, or buying something you've always wanted, rewarding yourself will motivate you to stick to your goals.

There is a quote from a movie: *All work and no play makes Jack go crazy*. This quote is put here not to make you think that working to achieve goals will make you crazy, but to remind you that acknowledging your own hard work is an important part of goal setting, so, acknowledge your hard work with a worthwhile token of appreciation.

For mid- and long-term goals, you may acknowledge your hard work when you reach major milestones. For example, in your quest to be a lawyer, you might reward yourself when you are accepted into law school, when you graduate from school, when you pass the Bar, and ultimately, when you land a position at a prestigious firm. Giving yourself rewards along the way will entice you to *keep on keeping on*.

GOALS CHANGE

Keep in mind that it's okay to change your goals. If you come to a point while working towards a goal and realize it is not really something that is going to fulfill you any more, it's o.k. to step back and start over. There is nothing wrong with admitting that a particular ambition is no longer right for you.

At times, this can be easier said than done. That is, it might be hard for you to let go of a goal you've put a lot of time and effort into. Even though it is something that you no longer want, you probably feel that all the effort you put in would go to waste if you quit now. This is good logic; however, if you devote yourself to an ambition and decide, for whatever reason, it no longer appeals to you, it is o.k. to re-evaluate and move on.

Don't think that the time and energy you put forth was wasted. The effort allowed you to build yourself up mentally. It also allowed you to gain knowledge and develop skills which you can now apply to your next endeavor. Trying something and realizing that it's not right for you is not the same as giving up.

Though this is not an excuse to give up because *the going got tough*. It is also not an excuse to jump from one endeavor to the next without a sense of commitment. Starting over with a new goal simply means there is no sense in continuing to do that which you do not enjoy. Remember that a goal is a guideline you set for yourself that is supposed to make your life better. If it doesn't do that, then jettison it and start over. After all, it is your life, and you get to live it only one time, so make the best of it.

These are the important considerations to keep in mind when working on your goals. To summarize, don't give up your goal if you miss a deadline or veer off course; reward your hard work, and start over if you change your mind about the goal.

The next time you face setbacks, don't get mired in frustration about things you can't control. Let go of wanting to see results right away. Stop forcing things to happen. Just focus on taking action, following your plan and keeping your eyes on the prize.

CONCLUSION

A journey of a thousand miles begins with a single step.—Lao Tzu

Many people find goal setting to be off-putting. To some, it is a tedious process that conjures up images of incessant work, unhappiness and endless toil. This may be because the *Now* generation has a short attention span. Perhaps it is because our culture has a low frustration tolerance. Whatever it is, the argument seems to be that you shouldn't have to accomplish goals to bring inner fulfillment. The question that arises is *what's wrong with being happy with the way things are?*

There is nothing wrong with finding happiness with your current situation. However, there is a reason you are reading this book. You are reading this book not because you want the same of what you already have. You want something more, something different, and something better. Whether that *something* is external change or internal transformation, setting goals, creating an action plan, and asserting affirmations are the most effective ways to get there.

Not to mention, the *don't worry, be happy* philosophy fails to acknowledge that most worthwhile accomplishments require some hard work. Since you have read this far, you are not of that ilk. You realize that hard work is not a dirty word and that setting reasonable goals is a good way to make progress. So whether you want to write a book, make more money, or get a college degree, set some goals.

Once you become comfortable with the process, goal achievement will become a pleasant experience for you, no matter what you want to attain. You'll know how to conquer your inner demons, face challenges head-on, and move quickly and precisely to your chosen outcome.

Through the process, you will strengthen and empower yourself more than you ever thought possible. You'll realize that your quality of life is completely within your control. More importantly, you will realize you need only follow a specific route to reach any destination you desire.

Then simply repeat the process to get to your next destination, and the next, and the one after that. It's as easy as lacing up your walking shoes and taking a stroll around the neighborhood. You may encounter some hills and valleys, perhaps a bit of rain or an aggressive dog or two, but just keep walking and you'll get to where you want to go.

To end, we leave you with a quote from Helmut Schmidt: *It must be born in mind that the tragedy of life doesn't lie in not reaching your goal. The tragedy lies in having no goal to reach.*

* * *

I hope you enjoyed learning about goal setting. As you can see, there is more to this tool than merely creating a list of wants and desires. If done correctly, it can give you a valuable blueprint for living a more fulfilled life. If you enjoyed the book, I would appreciate it if you can leave a positive review of it on Amazon or where you made the purchase. It will help others see the power and benefits of this technique.

If you found the advice useful, I highly recommend listening to the audio edition that is now available. Most people assume that just because they learn something new, that they will automatically put it to use. The mind doesn't work that way. No matter how profound, valuable, or critical new information might be to us, our recollection of it can fade very rapidly. In a few days to a few weeks, it can become a distant memory. Once that happens, we stop using what we've learned as we've forgotten about it.

So, if you really want to apply what you learned here, make sure to revisit the material regularly. An easy way to do that is to listen to the audio. With the audio, you can play it in the background or listen to it while doing other activities. Doing this once or twice a week will ensure the material stays fresh in your mind and keeps your motivation high at all times. You can find out how to get your free audio copy at www.bitly.com/goalaudio

As you learned in the section on affirmations, self-talk and visualization are vital to the goal setting process. If you'd like to learn more about these two techniques and take your ability to succeed to the next level, consider also reading:

The Art & Science of Visualization: A Practical Guide for Self-Help, Self-Healing, and Improving Other Areas of Yourself by Kam Knight

Self-Talk Your Way to Success by Kam Knight

Printed in Great Britain
by Amazon